Ten

Quick-Win Model

For Fast and Effective Service Delivery

A CMD PUBLICATION

National Library of Nigeria Cataloguing-in-Publication Data
Muoka, Charles Chuwkugozie
Ten Quick-Win Model for Fast and Effective Service Delivery
1, Customer Relations—Management.
1. Title.

HF5415.5. M 963	2017	658.812
ISBN: 978-978-55384-0-3	(pbk)	AACR2

Published in the Federal Republic of Nigeria by

CMM COMMUNICATIONS LIMITED

For more information and bulk orders, please contact the Marketing Department, CMM Communications Limited, Muoka Plaza, 18 Obinagu Road, Abakpa-Nike, PO Box 1139, Enugu, Nigeria.
Tel.: 0803-360-0825 E-mail:cmmcommunicationsltd@yahoo.com

The author, through the company CMM Communications Limited, is available to work with governments, institutions, and corporations desiring to reengineer and reenvision their quick-win strategies for faster and more effective service delivery and also for institutional or corporate seminars, workshops, and conferences and can be reached via e-mail at cmmcommunicationsltd@yahoo.com.

ISBN: 9785538400
ISBN 13: 9789785538403

To the Holy Spirit, my teacher and counselor, who guides me through all mysteries including that of this model and without whom I would have lacked the knowledge and understanding to have accomplished this work

To my dear friend and brother His Excellency Rt. Hon. Ifeanyi Ugwuanyi, executive governor, Enugu State, Nigeria, for whom the initial concept was developed and whose enthusiasm encouraged its further development into what readers now hold. And also for his resilient and genuine effort at repositioning and reinvigorating the economy of Enugu State that ensures prosperity of its citizens.

To all leaders, especially political leaders, who uphold the passion to deliberately meet the needs of their people in a high-quality way at all times

To all people who, through persistence in desiring that their needs be met by quality leaders, ensure that their leaders offer that quality

CONTENTS

FOREWORD

A Quick-Win is noted to be an action that speedily attract wide spread approval and acceptance of a target audience which confirms its satisfaction of the action. This book *Ten Quick-Win Model* ensures that this desired ultimate satisfaction is achieved fast and effectively.

Nearly everybody seems to know what a quick win is and what to do to achieve it, but only a few understand the how—the intricate processes of its execution for success. No wonder several governments, institutions, and corporations fail to achieve the set objectives and motives of their quick-win programs due to the application of inappropriate models for their execution.

This difficulty—which this book observes as a deterrent to a quick-win strategy and a challenge—is what this ten quick-win model (which is need based) addresses. It does this through its ten probing questions and procedures, which provide the needed insight, direction, practices, outcomes, applications, time frame, benefits, and evaluation matrix that ensure a successful quick-win plan.

This model contributes to the enhancement of the knowledge of quick-win effective execution procedures by practitioners, lessening chances of program failure and thereby encouraging more adventures into its exercise.

Hence, I highly recommend its adaptation by political leaders, CEOs, and program managers who are desirous of achieving the acceptance and approval of their quick-win plans by their target audience and accomplishment of their set motives and objectives of their programs for fast and effective service delivery for their practices.

Prof Fred O. Ede, PhD, fica, fiica, mnim
Professor of marketing and entrepreneurship
Former dean, faculty of management sciences
Enugu State University of Science & Technology
Enugu, Nigeria

ACKNOWLEDGEMENTS

The successful completion of this book is credited to the invaluable contributions of the following persons:

Dr. Egele A. E, my PhD academic adviser, who did the first appraisal of the book and guided its structure

Engr. Dr. Henry Morka, mechanical engineer and administrator; Mr. Adebayo Adekunle, printer; Mr. George Adama, banker; and Ms. Amara Nwankwo (Amray), musical artist

Mr. Ben Okoroafor, who not only did the graphic design but also made immense contributions in terms of review

Anonymous reviewers, for the assessment of the model in their various professions and for their insightful observations, which aided in improvement

Professor Nwaizugbo L., my PhD program supervisor, for his earnest review of the book and for his invaluable support

Professor Fred O. Ede , PhD, my academic mentor and the model project consultant who guided its final completion

EXECUTIVE SUMMARY

This book presents Ten Quick–Win Model for quick win practice. It explains quick-win to be action that speedily attract widespread acceptance and approval of a target market or audience as a result of providing visible valuable solution to its most immediate need. It lists qualities of a good quick-win as follows: it should convey a feeling of relief from apprehension of uncertainty and mixed expectation, thus creating the hope of better things to come; it should not be too expensive and should be such that could be quickly implemented in order not to lose the steam of attention; it should be captivating to stimulate and hold the immediate responsiveness of the target-audience so as to trigger the needed acceptance and approval.

These qualities of quick-win raise fundamental questions and concerns:

1. What is a successful quick win programme?
2. What are the benchmark criteria?
3. How should the programme be executed?
4. What should be its step-by-step process?
5. How should the needs be selected?
6. What techniques should be applied for the selection?
7. How would the approval and acceptance of the

programme by the target market or audience be guaranteed?
8. What time frame should be most apt for the execution of the programme?
9. What resource allocation would the programme require?

These critical issues burden every quick-win programme and often times are observed as deterrents. The challenge then is how to overcome these and deliver successful quick-win action.
This challenge is what this Ten Quick-Win Model through its offered set of ten needs-based probing questions and methodologies of application which ensures successful quick-win action, is believed to have overcome.

The book concludes that adoption of Ten Quick-Win Model and adherence to its methodologies of application for quick-win practice ensures its effective execution and success.

Hence, advocates that programme managers seeking to achieve acceptance and approval of their quick-win action by their target audience, and accomplishments of set objectives and motive(s) should adopt Ten Quick-Win Model for their practice.

CHAPTER ONE

1.1 INTRODUCTION

Quick win refers to action that speedily attract widespread acceptance and approval of a target market or audience as a result of providing visible valuable solution to its most immediate need. It is often times a bridge-gap to hold-down the audience from being frustrated while awaiting roll out of extensive programme. A good quick-win should convey a feeling of relief from apprehension of uncertainty and doubt of expectation; thus creating hope of better things to come. The action should not be too expensive and should be such that could be quickly implemented in order not to lose steam of attention.

Furthermore, it ought to be captivating to stimulate and hold immediate responsiveness of the target-audience so as to trigger needed acceptance and approval. This then provides needed reprieve of time, for an enhanced and effective planning, and roll-out of overall actions.

However, these raise some fundamental questions and concerns:

1. What is a successful quick win programme?
2. What are the benchmark criteria?
3. How should the programme be executed?
4. What should be its step-by-step process?

5. How should the needs be selected?

6. What technique should be applied for the selection?

7. How would the approval and acceptance of the programme by the target market be guaranteed?

8. What time frame should be most apt for the execution of the programme?

9. What resource allocation would the programme require?

These critical issues burden every quick win practice and often times are observed as deterrents. The challenge then is how to overcome these and deliver successful quick-win plan.

This challenge is what Ten Quick-Win Model through its offered ten needs-based probing questions and methodologies of application provide answers and directions to, which ensures effective and successful plan execution, and so overcomes the challenge.

The insights and directions – procedures, practices, outcomes, applications, time frame, benefits, and the evaluation matrix it provides are valuable tools in the hands of political leaders, chief executive officers (CEOs), chief financial officers (CFOs), heads of institutions and programme managers, and more. Its adoption for quick win programme ensures the realization of its objectives, motives and incentives for embarking on the quick-win. Therefore, its success should now encourage more adventures into quick-win programmes, and the target markets are better for it.

CHAPTER 2
ILLUSTRATION OF TEN QUICK-WIN MODEL

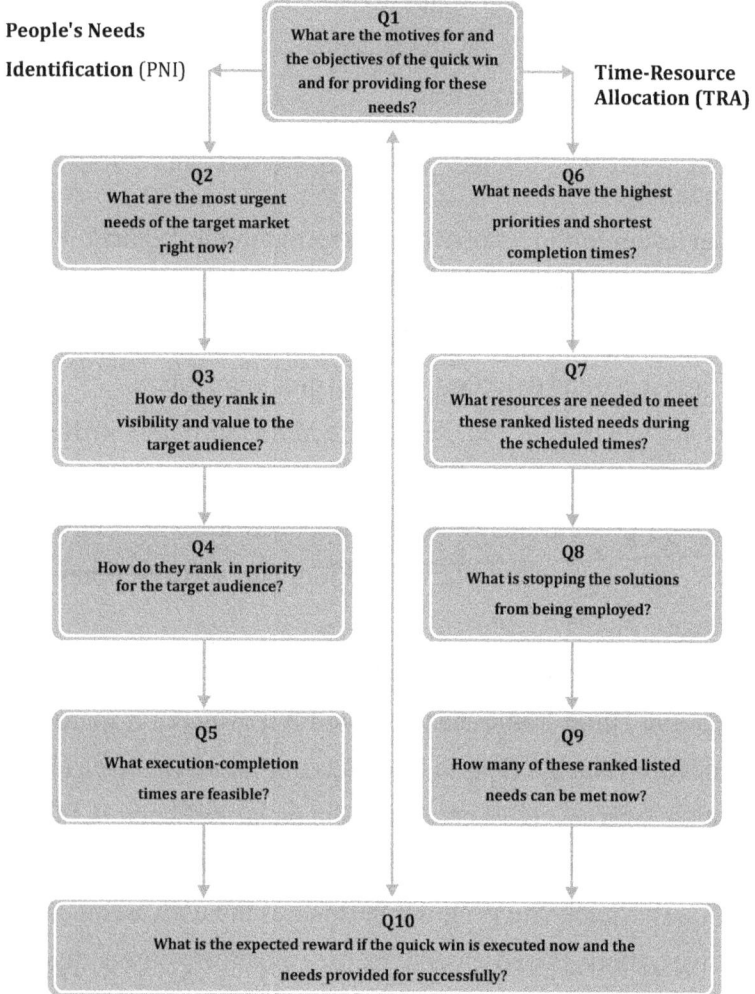

People's Needs

Identification (PNI)

Time-Resource
Allocation (TRA)

Q1
What are the motives for and the objectives of the quick win and for providing for these needs?

Q2
What are the most urgent needs of the target market right now?

Q6
What needs have the highest priorities and shortest completion times?

Q3
How do they rank in visibility and value to the target audience?

Q7
What resources are needed to meet these ranked listed needs during the scheduled times?

Q4
How do they rank in priority for the target audience?

Q8
What is stopping the solutions from being employed?

Q5
What execution-completion times are feasible?

Q9
How many of these ranked listed needs can be met now?

Q10
What is the expected reward if the quick win is executed now and the needs provided for successfully?

Key:
PNI:People's Needs Identification
TRA: Time-Resource Allocation
Q: Questions
Figure: Ten Quick-Win Model
Source: Author's Concept (2015)

PNI Q1: What are the motives and the objectives for the quick win and for providing these needs?
In this component, from the start, set clear motives—the core reasons for doing the quick win and measurable objectives—that the targets are intended to accomplish. These become the fulcrum of the quick-win program and the benchmark for evaluation of its success. A quick-win program without a preset motive and objectives is simply a ruse and a waste of resources as its outcome will be difficult to evaluate.

PNI Q2: What are the most urgent needs of the target market right now?
The list of the urgent needs of the target market should be itemized as a guide of the needs to be provided for by the quick-win program.

PNI Q3: How do they rank in visibility and value to the target market?
Adjust the prioritized list in accordance with their ranking in visibility and value to the target market or audience: this is the ranked list to be fine-tuned in terms of immediate perceived value to the target market or audience.

PNI Q4: How do they rank in priority to the target audience?
The list referenced above is further modified in accordance with their rank in priority or importance to the target market from highest priority to least. This ensures that the quick-win program targets and addresses the most important needs of the target

market. This ensures the program captures immediate attention as well as acceptance and approval.

PNI Q5: What are their most possible execution-completion times?
In accordance with the list, make a schedule of the most time it could take to completely execute each of the ranked needs.

TRA Q6: What needs with highest priority have shortest execution-completion times?
Further readjust the ranked list in accordance with their execution-completion times, starting with highest-priority needs with the shortest execution and completion times; then move on to those with the highest execution and completion times.

TRA Q7: What resources are available for the provision of these needs and within the scheduled time?
Resources and time are critical elements in the choice and timing of quick-win programs. Thus, determine the resources—capital, materials, and human resources—that will be required and that are available to provide for the needs and within the listed time.

TRA Q8: What are the constraints to their deployment for the provision of the ranked needs?
List the likely difficulties that may obstruct the due release of these resources for the provision of the needs, and proffer solutions to overcome them.

TRA Q9: How many of these ranked listed needs can be met now?
Determine the number of the ranked needs that can be provided for considering the available time and resources.

TRA Q10: What would be the expected reward if the quick win is executed now and the needs are provided successfully?
Determine the expected reward, the incentive for doing the quick win. This would be the expected positive outcome that confirms the approval and acceptance of the program by the target market or audience. It is seen as the zenith of a successful quick win as it fulfills its motives. The lure of this prize then becomes the momentum to drive the quick-win project to attain the set objectives. The reward also is a part of the criteria of evaluation of success.

CHAPTER 3

METHODOLOGY OF THE MODEL

The model methodology, procedures, and applications are listed below.

3.1 Sectors of Activities That Need the Model

- Governments: executive, legislative, and judicial branches and MDAs (ministries, departments, and agencies)
- Political parties
- Corporations
- Institutions
- Religious bodies
- Civil society organizations (CSOs) and clubs
- Individuals
- Researchers

3.2 Outcomes of Research and Applications

3.2.1 SITUATIONS IN WHICH THE ABOVE-LISTED SECTORS WOULD REQUIRE THE MODEL

3.2.1a *Political Situations for Governments and Political Parties*

- The emergence of a new political leader—president, governor, or council chair—with the urgent need to show leadership competence, true understanding of the critical issues at stake, and direction to the people, who do not want drawn - out programmes.
- A sitting political leader experiencing loss of confidence of the people
- A sitting political leader desiring to continuously hold the

attention and admiration of the relevant public
- A newly appointed political-office holder—for example, a minister, board chair, director general, or commissioner—who needs to prove competence to the public to retain confidence after appointment
- A political-office holder needing to restore confidence after losing it
- A newly elected political office holder—for example, a parliamentarian seeking electoral support
- A politician preparing for an election needing the attention and acceptance of the public
- A politician who has been disgraced but is positioned for a comeback
- A politician seeking a political appointment and needing to show competence to the public
- A politician who needs to remain visible and relevant to the public
- A politician who has just lost an election and needs to still remain visible and relevant to the public
- An unknown and aspiring politician who needs to become visible and relevant to the public
- A political leader with the need to sustain a stronghold on his or her following
- Anyone with a need to make a political statement—to show uncommon political savvy, ingenuity, and creativity—to demonstrate unusual knowledge and understanding of people's needs or circumstance
- A political party preparing for an election and needing to win the support of the electorate
- A political party that wins an election and needs to show

gratitude to the voters for their support
- A political party that loses an election and needs repositioning for a comeback

3.2.1b Corporate Situations for Businesses

The business situations that require the model include the following:
- Leaders in transition to new roles with an urgent need to show competency through an early result to the relevant public; benefactors who appointed a leader into the office who need reassurance of the leader's ability to handle responsibility; teammates assessing whether to place their confidence in the new leader; and the peer group assessing equality of the leader to their rank (Van Buren and Safferstone 2009)
- Corporate social responsibility
- Staff welfare
- Customer rewards
- Product development

3.2.1c Institutional Situations

Institutions would require ten quick-win model in determining the following:
- Staff welfare
- Services development
- Target audience services advocacy

3.2.1d Religious Situations

Similarly, religious institutions would require ten quick-win model when they are faced with certain decisions:
- Target audience services development

- Services promotion
- Priests/pastor welfare
- Staff welfare

3.2.1e Civil Society Organizations (CSOs) and Club Situations

The CSOs and clubs would require the model in deciding the following:
- Staff welfare
- Target audience services development
- Target audience services advocacy

3.2.1f Individual Situations in Homes or in Making Personal Business Decisions

- Community support activities for visibility and relevance in society
- Family and extended family support actions
- Club/society support actions for visibility and relevance
- Choice of business opportunities
- Musical artist developing a new song for a music label
- Author writing a new book for publication
- Film producer with a range of films to choose from

3.2.1g Research Situations

The model could be used by researchers for further research development to test the hypothesis.

3.3 Procedures for Using the Model

Below is a guide to the best way to apply the model to achieve effective and successful execution:

1. Approve and adopt ten quick-win model in the execution of a quick-win program.

2. If a quick-win program has already been embarked upon, then benchmark the program to the ten quick-win model test to evaluate its success potential.

3. If it fails the benchmarking test, then discard the program as a waste of resources and time as it may not accomplish the objectives, motives and rewards for embarking on the program. If it passes the test, then uphold the program to its logical completion.

4. If none is already in execution, then commission very quickly a short survey that could be obtained from either primary or secondary data to help establish the needs of the people.

5. The structure of the questionnaire should also include the target market's needs rankings in accordance with their visibility, value, and priority.

6. Use the obtained data, and follow the sequence of the model to record their rankings in visibility and value and then in priority.

7. Establish their completion times.

8. Adjust the ranked list to start with needs of highest priority and the shortest completion times and then move to those with long completion times.

9. List out the resources that may be needed to execute each of the needs for completion. Further readjust the ranked list of items in accordance with their resource needs, starting from needs with the least resource requirements to those with the highest.

10. Determine the likely constraints on the deployment of these resources, and proffer solutions to them.

11. In consideration of the available resources and time, use

the ranked prioritized list of item to determine the number of the needs that can be done now. Record the needs for execution in that order.

12. List out the teams or subunits that would be involved in their execution, either directly or remotely.

13. Identify the implementation team for these units now.

14. Formally engage the implementation team.

15. Let the team go to work immediately to assemble the urgently needed data to ensure that the schedules of the program execution will be met.

16. Ensure appropriate funding and all needed support to the team to guarantee their ability to successfully execute the assignment on schedule.

17. Ensure commission execution.

18. Enforce acts' evaluation and rewards system for the team.

19. Evaluate performance using the achievement of the set objectives, motives and rewards as key benchmarks.

20. Celebrate the success(Case2012).

3.4 Time Frame of the Model

Quick wins are normally based on a short timeline (Van Buren and Safferstone 2009). Sometimes they are to help forestall the target market from being frustrated while awaiting execution of extensive programs. Hence, the following time schedule is hereby recommended:

· Seven-day quick wins
· Thirty-day quick wins
· Sixty-day quick wins
· One-hundred–day quick wins

Performance Evaluation

During and after the execution of the quick-win program, it will be necessary to assess whether the set motives, objectives and rewards for embarking on the plan have been realized. The following procedures should be used to assess its performance.

3.5.1 THE APPROVAL AND ACCEPTANCE OF THE PROGRAM BY THE TARGET MARKET OR AUDIENCE

The overall reactions of the target audience on the commencement of the quick-win program execution indicate their acceptance and approval or otherwise. Positive reactions of the majority of the target market indicate acceptance and approval of the program while negative reactions indicate disapproval and rejection. This can easily be established through simple questionnaire-based research immediately at the start of the program execution.

3.5.1a Case-Study Example

The New Buhari Government in Nigeria, elected on the platform of change and in effort to have a quick win with the Nigerian people to sustain and advance the acceptance it is enjoying, has made a daring move in determination to kill the corruption present in the country since its foundation and announces as follows:

- ✍ Henceforth, MDAs are barred from awarding contracts without financial provision for their execution.
- ✍ No project not earlier listed in the yearly budget can be executed from the budgetary provision of that year.
- ✍ The government will fulfill its commitments to all on going contracts as listed and provided for in the yearly budget.
- ✍ It remains illegal to misappropriate funds—transferring

funds provided for specific projects in the budget to another, thereby causing project failures and financial crises in the financial sector(which has resulted in several business failures, sudden health challenges among contractors, and untimely deaths of some who could not withstand the pressure)

3.5.1b. Government Sets Three Objectives for the Quick Win

- To demonstrate to the Nigerian people unequivocally its firm commitment to kill corruption right from its foundation in the economy of the country.
- To sustain, boost, and advance the change euphoria already widespread across the country.
- To salvage and restrengthen several corporations and enterprises(SMEs)that are already dead or in danger of extinction due to non payment of their due certificates and delayed funding of their projects through budget misappropriation by MDAs

3.5.1c. Government Sets the Motive for the Quick Win

Similarly, the government also sets the motive for executing the quick-win program: to boost and sustain the perception of the president by the Nigerian people as a credible, courageous, and incorruptible true agent of change.

3.5.1d Performance Evaluation of the Case-Study Example

The performance evaluation of the study example could be assessed by checking if the above-mentioned pronouncements of the government are immediately followed up by all necessary directives needed for their instant implementation. This could be as follows:

- The secretary to the federal government (SGF) immediately mandates within twenty-four hours a circular directing the head of service to the compliance with the new directive and a task force set up to oversee its implementation.

In addition, the task force identifies such misappropriations, especially in the past twenty-four years.

- If the MDAs announce and demonstrate immediate compliance to the directive leading to simultaneous widespread approval and acceptance of governmental action by Nigerian people—as can be easily confirmed through across-board endorsement of the action by various stakeholders, such as construction firms; financial institutions; the Nigeria Society of Engineers (NSE); the Manufacturers Association of Nigeria (MAN); the Chamber of Commerce, Industry, Mines and Agriculture (CCIMA); the Association of Small and Medium Enterprises Organizations of Nigeria (ASMEON); the International Donor Agencies; the Nigeria Labour Congress (NLC); the Civil Society Organizations (CSOs); religious organizations; the Nigeria Union of Journalists (NUJ); the Nigeria Bar Association (NBA); and the Student Unions of Nigeria (SUN)—then the action is said to have received a positive response, boosting change in reality in the country.

However, if otherwise, the action will have failed, diminishing the euphoria of change—casting it as a ruse with a consequent loss of credibility in the person of Buhari and deep regret as to his choice as president.

Further, beyond the endorsements, following the full implementation of the policy and the testimonials of the benefitting contractors through receipt of their duly approved payments, evidencing the change in the government's procurement process (which would result in restoration of dead and near-dead businesses), the change euphoria that had received a boost is then sustained. The continual implementation of change in the procurement system deepens and advances the change reality and then becomes ingrained in the people, bringing about a real attitude change in the country as the government is then seen to be leading by example. This perception by the people that the government of Buhari is leading by example is what would drive the people to continue to perceive the president as a truly credible, courageous, and incorruptible agent of change, thus accomplishing the motive for the quick win.

3.5.2 How to Avoid Program Disapproval and Possible Rejection

Do the simple questionnaire-based research before the start of the quick-win program to properly establish the true needs of the target market. Ensure that the relevant public of the target market constitutes part of the respondents to the research. This would guarantee that their opinions and input are well captured and used in the program-planning process.

3.5.3 The Attainment of the Set Objectives

The accomplishment of the set objectives, especially within the scheduled time, confers success status on the plan. So, benchmark the given example on attainment of the set objectives:

✍   **Objective 1:** The full implementation of the new directive on procurement by the MDAs being part of the foundation of corruption rot in Nigeria will to a great extent reduce the practices of corruption in the country and so accomplish the first objective.

✍   **Objective 2:** The sustaining, boosting, and advancing of the "change"euphoria across the country will be achieved by the full and continuous implementation of the "new change" in the procurement process by the MDAs.

·   **Objective 3:** The testimonials of the benefitting contractors and other participants in the procurement process will confirm that change has indeed taken root, thus confirming achievement of the third objective.

3.5.4 The Fulfillment of the Motive

The sustained implementation of the new directive to MDAs in the government procurement process and prosecution of all defaulters without exception would endear the government of Buhari to the Nigerian people and cause them to perceive the president as a truly credible, courageous, and incorruptible agent of change, thus accomplishing the motive for the quick win.

CHAPTER FOUR

BENEFITS OF THE MODEL

- It examines the motive and the expected reward for a quick- win program.

- It then helps to set clearly the identified objectives and expected reward to avoid ambiguity

- The reward then becomes the driving force of the motives and objectives, which propels the quick-win program to its effective execution and success.

- Because the model is need based, it reveals the true needs of the people in accordance with their priorities and preferences, thus ensuring the achievement of the set objectives and reward and thereby avoiding program failure.

- It helps from the onset in understanding the program time and resource needs and ensures their apt management, thus guaranteeing program success.

- It provides answers and directions to the fundamental questions and concerns that burden quick-win plan execution.

- It overcomes the inherent challenges of intricate processes prevalent in the execution of quick-win programs.

- The insights, directions, and evaluation matrix it offers are valuable tools in the hands of quick-win planners.

- It helps to ensure the realization of the objectives and rewards of a quick-win plan.

- Its success encourages more ventures into quick-win activities.

CHAPTER 5

CONCLUSION

The adoption of ten quick-win model and adherence to its methodology of application for quick-win activities ensure its effective execution and success.

Therefore, political and business leaders and program managers seeking to attract the approval and acceptance of a target market or audience for a quick-win program and achieve set motives and objectives for fast and effective service delivery should adopt ten quick-win model.

REFERENCES

Case, Gary. 2012. "Pink Elephant-Process Improvement Quick Wins: World Leaders in Transforming IT Services." http://www.pinkelephant.com/en-US/About-Pink/Contact/2013/last accessed: 25 (September).

Van Buren, M. E., and T. Safferstone. 2009. "Quick Win Paradox: Change Management." Harvard Business Review (January).

About the Author

Charles Muoka is a native of Agulu in A n a o c h a Local Government Area of Anambra State, Nigeria and was born in Agulu in 1964.

He holds Ph.D in Marketing from Ebonyi State University, Abakaliki, Ebonyi State, and his thesis research topic was *brand attributes of political candidates and sustainable electoral success in Nigeria, and* M.Sc. in Marketing-Public Relations Management and Post Graduate Diploma in Business Administration and Marketing- Public Relation Management from University of Nigeria Nsukka, Enugu State. He also holds B.Sc. in Marketing, Purchasing and Supply Management from Enugu State University of Science and Technology (ESUT). Enugu, Enugu State, Nigeria.

He is the Founder of CMM Group with interests   in manufacturing, trading, construction and publishing and has extensive experiences in both public and private sectors.

Dr. Muoka is highly travvelled (Europe, USA, Asia and Africa). He is happily married to the love of his life Nkechi Elizabeth and they have an adorable son Charles Michael Chukwugozie Jr. - a cum Laude Honours Graduate of Bowie State University, Maryland, USA.

www.ingramcontent.com/pod-product-compliance
Lightning Source LLC
Chambersburg PA
CBHW071145200326
41519CB00022B/6950